Zero Limits: Breaking Out of Your Comfort Zone

By Craig Beck

Copyright Craig Beck Media Limited 2016

The free companion downloads for these books are available to download at www.craigbeck.com

Chapters

Introduction
Chapter 1 — Fear-a-phobia
Chapter 2 — V is for Victim
Chapter 3 — I Want You, But I Don't Need You
Chapter 4 — Forgive Yourself First
Chapter 5 — The Illusion of Permanency
Chapter 6 — Fear, Your New BFF
Chapter 7 — Outcomes & Labels

Introduction

Your comfort zone is a beautiful place, so sheltered, warm and secure. But we've been tricked! This place that we all tend to default to is nothing but an illusionary safe haven… for nothing ever grows inside the comfort zone.

No one who ever lived an exceptional life did so from inside this barren and sterile place. If you honestly want to achieve your true potential, then the first thing you must do is pack your bags and leave comfort town.

In Zero Limits, bestselling personal development author Craig Beck shows you how to dramatically change your perception of risk and fear, so you can easily smash right through your current self-imposed limitations. If you follow this unique path and start to live a fearless life—way beyond what you currently believe you are capable of—amazing things will start happening. You will:

• Achieve your goals and ambitions faster than you ever thought possible.
• Develop unshakable self-confidence and self-esteem.
• Discover rapid personal and professional progression.
• Experience more abundance flowing into your life.
• Live the life most people can only dream of.

Chapter One – Fear-a-phobia

"Remembering that I'll be dead soon is the most important tool I've ever encountered to help me make the big choices in life.

"Almost everything—all external expectations, all pride, all fear of embarrassment or failure—these things just fall away in the face of death, leaving only what is truly important.

"Remembering that you are going to die is the best way I know to avoid the trap of thinking you have something to lose. You are already naked. There is no reason not to follow your heart.

"No one wants to die. Even people who want to go to heaven don't want to die to get there. And yet, death is the destination we all share. No one has ever escaped it, and that is how it should be, because death is very likely the single best invention of life. It's life's change agent. It clears out the old to make way for the new." - Steve Jobs

Back when I first started out in the media industry as a cocky seventeen-year-old boy, I remember once being interviewed by a local newspaper. I had just been appointed as the new breakfast presenter for Radio Wyvern, in Worcestershire—a town near the southern Welsh border with England. At the time I was the youngest morning show host in the country and the pressure was on me to not only mature fast, but also to quickly demonstrate that I was worthy of the risk some poor misguided program director had taken by putting such a total newbie in this enormous position. The newspaper article had been arranged as a favor for the boss, so it was only ever going to be a light hearted affair. I didn't need to be too careful what I said because the journalist had been asked to write something that was nothing more than a complimentary commercial for my new breakfast show. The depth and weight of those questions would hardly tax me further than a query about my favorite color.

It quickly became apparent that I was going to be given twenty harmless, if somewhat inane, questions to provide material for an article about me that they would probably bury somewhere on page thirty seven, somewhere near the classified ads for lost pets and surgical support stockings. I answered each question quickly and honestly, while the journalist would listen to my reply, sigh and scribble something down on his note pad. After four or five questions I realized that I was boring the guy to death. Hey, I was seventeen years old, nobody had ever told me how to speak to the press, or even how to answer trivia about myself.

I decided I was going to have to spice up my answers and try to be a little more of a personality. After all, I was guessing that was all this poor guy was clinging to for ammunition to write what was looking to be the most tedious piece of copy of his career. After a few more questions, I felt like I was doing a little better. The journalist had smiled once and raised his eyebrows a few times. I decided that meant I was either doing great or really bad, and I wouldn't know for sure until I saw the actual newspaper the next day, or got called to the boss' office for the hair dryer treatment.

Question twelve was 'what is your biggest fear.' I looked him square in the eye and paused a moment. Then, in my best Roger Moore style, I raised one eyebrow, and said, "Fear is my only fear—everything else is child's play."

This answer immediately made me want to vomit. It was so putrid and contrived that every year on the anniversary of this interview, the same gut wrenching, bile-inducing sensation came over me. It happened for many years that followed, like some sort of divine punishment for saying something so pretentious and appalling.

Here I am twenty-five years later sitting on a train to London, and for some reason that memory is as fresh as it was the day I uttered such trite nonsense. Shockingly, I have now come to believe it may have leapt from the grey, murky bog of my mind because it may actually have been true. Hold on, I am aware the premise doesn't defend against such wanton pomposity, and I probably still deserve a good slap about the chops. Nonetheless, 'fear' is what I have come to recognize as the single biggest element that prevents me (and everybody else) from reaching our true potential and really living the life of our dreams. It is not logic, responsibility or contentment that keeps us trapped in underachievement; it is fear that holds the key to our jail cell.

Human behavior appears to be complex and multilayered, but in reality, it comes down to two simple elements. All human motivation is essentially a binary process, meaning that we are moved to either do something or avoid doing something by a single switch in our head being in one position or the other. All decisions, actions, and deeds are made as a result of us either avoiding fear or pursuing pleasure, and that is pretty much it. The reason for everything we do comes down to this simple premise.

We can spend hours debating the issue (as I have done many times before) but trust me on this one, even the apparently self-sacrificing actions of a parent for their child are still motivated by the emotions of fear and pleasure.

In the case of self-esteem and confidence, the fear that prevents us from performing as we could is 99.9% misplaced. Of course, sometimes the fear we feel most definitely has a place and I am not suggesting you ignore that little voice in your head that suggests you can't safely jump from one tall building to another. The fear you feel just before you do your first parachute jump is a process of the human mind operating exactly as it should. Making you feel afraid in these moments is a form of self-preservation. It is the brain's way of saying, 'hey if you continue doing what you are doing, there is a very good chance you will die, and you will most likely take me along with you!'

But the fear that suggests that you are not attractive enough to talk to the hot girl is a misfire of this process. The gut-twisting anxiety you experience as you step up to make a presentation to the whole office is this life-saving feature of the human mind misunderstanding the situation and trying to force you to exit an environment it has incorrectly judged to be dangerous.

Confidence, or rather the lack of it, is a simple throw back to our earlier times as hunter-gatherers. Putting it another way, we are witnessing and experiencing the time lag of evolution trying to catch up with and adapt to what modern life involves. The life of a human being in the western world today has changed so dramatically over the last few hundred years that it is almost incomparable to what our forefathers had to endure. Today we get upset and feel like we have had a bad day if we can't find a parking space in the lot or spill our latte on our favorite t-shirt.

Compared to the life-threatening events that happened on a daily basis to the generations that went before us, our problems are embarrassingly trivial. As relatively recently as the 1800's, the average life expectancy of a human male living in the United Kingdom was 39 years. With disease, unsafe working conditions and vigilantly justice commonplace, someone at my tender age of 40 would be considered an old man. Perhaps my children have been correct all along when they insist I am incapable of appreciating their musical taste because I am so decrepit.

Bearing in mind that evolution is a painfully slow process that takes hundreds of thousands of years to make even the smallest adaptations to the design of our species, you can see why it is struggling to keep up with our rapidly changing modern lifestyles. While Apple may bring out a new model of its products every year, Mother Nature does not!

Back when we were at constant risk of being attacked by not only wild animals but also our fellow uncivilized man, the human mind developed systems to try and keep us alive despite the inherent danger around us. Perhaps the most famous of these is what we call the 'flight or fight' response.

When our fight or flight response is activated, sequences of nerve cells fire and potent chemicals like adrenaline, noradrenaline, and cortisol are released into our bloodstream. If you want to see how dramatic these chemicals are, get food poisoning and watch what happens. I can tell you from recent experience that your body uses these neuro chemicals to make you dance like you are nothing more than a puppet on a string. When the body detects you have ingested something dangerous, like rotten food or too much alcohol, it needs to force you to evacuate the offending material, and it doesn't want to waste time debating this with you. Vast amounts of chemicals are released by your central nervous system that makes you feel incredibly ill, almost to the point where you feel like you are going to die. The next thing you know you are holding onto the toilet bowl as your life depended on it, screaming projectile vomit into the water. As a reward for doing as you were told, the body now releases mind-bending amounts of dopamine, which has the effect of making you feel instantly better—almost high. I don't advise you to experience food poisoning to verify this for yourself, just trust me.

My apologies, a rather unpleasant tangent sidetracked me there for a moment, though it was a good example. Now, getting back to how the mind instigates the flight or fight response. These patterns of neuro reactions and chemical releases force our body to undergo a series of very dramatic changes. Our respiratory rate increases. Blood is shunted away from our digestive tract and directed into our muscles and limbs, which require extra energy and fuel for running, fighting or maybe even both.

- Our pupils dilate
- Our awareness intensifies
- Our sight sharpens
- Our impulses quicken
- Our perception of pain diminishes.
- Our immune system mobilizes.
- We become prepared physically and psychologically for fight or flight.
- We scan and search our environment, looking for the enemy or threat.

When our fight or flight system is activated, we tend to perceive everything in our environment as a possible threat to our survival. By its very nature, the fight or flight system bypasses our rational mind—where our better thought out beliefs exist, and instead it moves us into "attack" mode. This state of alertness causes us to perceive almost everything in our world as a possible threat to our survival. As such, we tend to see everyone and everything as a possible enemy. Like airport security during a terrorist threat, we are on the lookout for every possible danger.

We may overreact to the slightest comment. Our fear is exaggerated. Our thinking is distorted. We see everything through the filter of possible danger. We narrow our focus to those things that can harm us. Fear becomes the lens through which we see the world.

Our fight or flight response is designed to protect us from the proverbial saber tooth tigers that once lurked in the woods and fields around us, threatening our physical survival. On those occasions when our actual physical survival is threatened, there is no greater response to have on our side. When activated, the fight or flight response causes a surge of adrenaline and other stress hormones to pump through our body. This surge is the inexplicable force responsible for mothers lifting cars off their trapped children, and for firemen heroically running into blazing buildings to save endangered victims. The surge of adrenaline infuses us with heroism and courage at times when we are called upon to protect and defend the lives and values we cherish.

While this protective routine still has a valid place in our lives, it does not need to be activated nearly as frequently as it is, and certainly not in situations that lack true danger, such as making a PowerPoint presentation at work!

But I think that 'flight or fight' is an incorrect moniker for this instinctive response to stress. There is a missing F in that much-quoted saying. Actually, the more common reaction in situations deemed to be high risk is not to fight or flee, but rather to freeze.

Fight, Flight or FREEZE

I am sure at times you have felt that 'deer in the headlights' sensation, where you know what is expected of you but somehow just can't bring yourself to move. There are no mistakes in nature and obviously removing your conscious ability to move, is a feature designed by evolution. If a giant brown bear enters your immediate environment and your subconscious programming decides that the best chance you have to remain alive is to play dead, then the last thing it wants is your pesky (and weak) conscious mind to have a say on the decision. So it locks you down, and despite how much you want to move, you find that it is virtually impossible.

When you freeze before making a speech or feel like your tongue has been paralyzed the very moment the beautiful woman starts to talk to you, this is simply the mind misreading the situation as dangerous and firing off one of your self-preservation routines. Of course, the big question is, how do you stop doing this?

The answer to this question and the beginning of a life full of abundance and success lies in the following pages. All I ask at this point is that you don't try to skip ahead and find the magic bullet. You will find no such thing; there is no one sentence that can independently build your confidence. Success, as with everything else in life, is not about the final destination. It is all about the journey.

What I have discovered in life is that pretty much anything worth having is just slightly outside your comfort zone. Whether it's launching your own business, winning the league in your chosen sport, getting the career you have dreamed of or ending up with the man or woman who makes you feel like you just won the lottery every moment you are with them. None of these things are inside your comfort zone, they all require you to stretch and grow before you can reach them. As most people know, the walls of your comfort zone are made of a very strong material called fear. To smash through these barriers you have to stare fear straight in the eyes and charge ahead regardless.

Fear (false evidence appearing real) is just an illusion, and I don't just mean certain types of fear. You might quite reasonably argue that the anxiousness you feel when you stand on the top of a tall building is a very valuable sensation to experience at that moment. Of course, sometimes fear serves you in the short term, but the biggest problem we have as an intelligent species is that we believe that we have something to lose. The quote from Steve Jobs that I opened this book with is perhaps the most profound paragraph I have ever heard, and for that reason, you will find it quoted verbatim in many of my books. You are going to die, not one of us is getting out of this alive. One day everything you ever worried about will become irrelevant dust. You are already naked, you always have been, and there is not a single reason why you should not be following your dreams and living a life full of happiness, peace, and purpose!

When this ride is over nobody is going to mention the day you risked it all and unsuccessfully went after that big promotion at work, nobody will recall the day you threw caution to the wind and gambled with rejection by approaching that beautiful girl you saw in the street. All this stuff is only significant to your ego.

Law of attraction books like The Secret tells you that if you want to be rich then act like a rich person, think like a rich person and express gratitude for your wealth before it arrives. I am telling you this will never work UNLESS you believe you deserve it.

When you consider what you want in life, ask yourself this, does it lie beyond a wall of fear you are never going to cross? If so, then you will always use the divine power within you to hold your dreams just slightly out of reach. No matter how positive your thinking gets, no matter how many affirmations you make or how much gratitude you express, fear is going to prevent you from manifesting magic into your life.

In this book, you will make friends with fear. I will show you how I recognize fear, not as a warning or obstacle, but rather as an indicator of an opening window of opportunity. I have learned that when I am afraid to do something, the universe is telling me clearly and specifically what I have to do next. Fear is a very strong sign to me that an opportunity to learn, develop and grow has arrived. What most people see as an obstacle, I see as the most powerful gift anyone can get, and I am going to give the same paradigm to you, starting today.

Chapter Two - V is for Victim

"Let me tell you something you already know. The world ain't all sunshine and rainbows. It's a very mean and nasty place, and I don't care how tough you are, it will beat you to your knees and keep you there permanently if you let it. You, me, or nobody is gonna hit as hard as life.

"But it ain't about how hard you hit. It's about how hard you can get hit and keep moving forward; how much you can take and keep moving forward. That's how winning is done! Now, if you know what you're worth, then go out and get what you're worth. But you gotta be willing to take the hits, and not pointing fingers saying you ain't where you wanna be because of him, or her, or anybody. Cowards do that and that ain't you. You're better than that!

"I'm always gonna love you, no matter what. No matter what happens. You're my son and you're my blood. You're the best thing in my life. But until you start believing in yourself, you ain't gonna have a life." - Rocky Balboa

I want to tell you about Katie, I am sure you know her already, perhaps not the same Katie, but certainly 'a Katie.' Poor Katie drew a bad hand in life; she didn't do great at school because, as she tells the story, the teachers were idiots. She always dreamed of a cool apartment overlooking the sea, with a little dog called Jack. Unfortunately, because her boss is an asshole she has to rent a crummy little studio apartment in a rough part of town, and since the landlord is a total douche and doesn't allow pets, she is not even allowed to have a dog.

Talk to Katie yourself, and she will tell you how unfair life is and how she deserves so much more. Way more than 'so and so,' 'whose it,' or 'what's her name,' yet they have everything she wants. She will tell you that nobody understands her and that all her friends are two-faced bitches who are out to cause as much trouble as possible.

Is it conceivable that Katie just got an unlucky break in life? Is there any chance that she is correct in her assessment? Let's put it this way. Move over Mother Teresa; there is more chance of Donald Trump becoming a Saint than of Katie being accurate in her assessment of why she is not living the life she says she wants. Katie is a victim, and these victims are everywhere—we can't move for them. These are the people that believe life owes them something, and they often spend an entire lifetime furious that the neighbor got yet another new car, or so and so got promoted at work.

Victims not only suck the energy out of their own lives but do the same for anyone who comes close enough to get caught up in their vortex of doom. I call them mood Hoovers and I am almost certain you can think of at least a few people who fit perfectly into this description. Let's first talk about how you deal with this trait in other people, and then I want you to look within. We'll have a little honesty session and examine areas of your life where you may have adopted the roll of victim because it is easier than facing the hard truth.

How do you help a victim? The short answer? You can't because they don't want to be helped. They like being the victim; it gives them a convenient explanation as to why their life blows chunks. On their deathbed you could ask them 'why didn't you live the life you were truly capable of,' and they will have enough plausible deniability to stubbornly point at something or someone and say 'because of that.' All the time they are pointing a finger of blame at everything and everyone else around them, they are blissfully unaware that they have three fingers pointed right back at them. It is frustrating to care about this type of a victim because you can see the huge untapped potential in them, but they cannot. When they look in the mirror, all they see is someone who has been badly treated by life.

If they are a friend or family member, perhaps even your son or daughter, you will desperately try to help them see the truth, but in my experience all you will end up doing is expending vast amounts of time, money and energy to get precisely nowhere with them. The harsh reality is this; we are all divine creations. We each have a fragment of God embedded within us, and we all have the power to perform our own miracles. If we take decisive action and flow with the universe instead of kicking violently trying to go back up stream, we can manifest breathtakingly amazing lives for ourselves. Victims have this power too, but they choose to ignore it.

How to spot a victim

Victims have reasons, lots of them and often they seem like entirely logical and plausible explanations.

- I am ill because the doctor gave me the wrong medicine.
- I am poor because my boss is a jerk.
- I got fired because I am a woman.
- I became redundant because I am black.
- They won't employ me because I am white.
- I can't quit drinking because it's the only pleasure I have left.
- I am too stressed to stop smoking.

The list goes on and on, and all of it is 100% bullshit. There are four certainties in this life. You will be born, you will die, and in between, you will pay taxes and life will repeatedly knock you down. As Rocky Balboa says, 'Ain't nothing going to hit as hard as life.' Getting knocked down is not bad luck any more than turning on the tap and getting water could be considered good luck. Life is getting knocked down; the choice is getting back up again, looking it in the eye and saying 'is that all you got, hit me again, but this time put some effort into it!' The reason you can't help the victims is because when they do get knocked down, they love it. It gives them what they want, an excuse not to get back up again, and proves the point they've been trying to make all along. They are like boxers who are too tired to keep fighting and are hoping for one decent punch so they can fall with dignity and stay the hell down until the referee counts ten.

Exercise

Stop reading for ten minutes and think about the victims in your life. Ask yourself who they are, how long they have been there and most importantly, how much time you are spending trying to make them feel better. Which, in case you hadn't noticed, is like trying to push oil uphill. Once you are clear about who these people are, I want you to make a conscious decision to spend less and less time in their company—until they are no longer a part of your life. That's right; I am asking you to fire the mood Hoovers in your life. You can't help them, and they are not helping you, so it's time for them to go.

There is a way to help, but it is almost certainly not what you are doing at the moment. If dumping them out of your life is not possible, or you are not comfortable doing that, then at least reduce the amount of time you spend with them and use the cleaning method I describe in detail in Magic part 4. To do this, you have to accept responsibility for your share of the problem. The fact that this person's victim mentality is present in your manifestation of the universe means that it exists within you at a subconscious level as well. Use the healing meditation of Ho'oponopono to clean the program within you, and you will both reap the benefits.

But wait… what if you are the victim?

Are you a victim? This is a pretty easy question to answer; think of something in your life that you are not happy with. For example, you need more money. Now with that problem in mind, explain to yourself why this is your current situation. If you find you have answers and excuses readily available (such as because my boss keeps overlooking me for promotion), then you are operating in a victim mindset around this topic. If your response is more positive and places responsibility on your shoulders. Then you are in an abundance mindset (for example—I took a pay cut to change the direction of my career, but I know if I give this new job 100% I am going to earn far more than I would have in the old role).

Having an abundance mindset always starts with you taking 100% responsibility. Let me give you an example from my own life. In 2007, I bought a villa in Cyprus. I didn't know it at the time, but I was investing at possibly the worst time in the last century. Property prices were hugely overinflated, and there was a mad rush of eager buyers trying to get in on what was being touted as a gold rush. Realtors promised anyone who would listen that you could easily double your money within a few short years. I had always wanted to live in the sunshine by the sea, so I went all in. Three months after I collected the keys to my property the Lehman Brothers collapsed, and the whole western world went into a financial meltdown.

Overnight, my property lost 40% of its value, but that was irrelevant, as the whole market had evaporated. Due to a concrete explosion over the past few years, the tiny island of Cyprus found itself with thousands and thousands of new build property and absolutely no buyers to be seen. To make matters worse, I had taken a mortgage in Swiss francs on the advice of the bank. Because Switzerland was considered a safe haven outside the crashing dollar, pound, and euro, their currency value went through the roof. My mortgage payments tripled overnight.

Whose fault is this disastrous investment? The victim would say it's the realtor for advising me badly; it's the bank for selling me a volatile product or any other number of villains that could be pointed at and labeled as the 'fault' behind this mess. But at the point where you create an excuse, you become a reaction to life. You are a passenger who is responding to the events of life that are thrust upon you. Conversely, when you accept 100% responsibility for the events around you, then you are in the driver's seat. Let me tell you when you are alone in a runaway car, the last place you want to be sitting is in the passenger seat.

Here are my thoughts about the house in Cyprus. It is my responsibility, I created it and I will solve it. I don't believe it was a mistake; I believe it is a blessing here in my life to push me in a specific direction, to challenge me, to teach me and ultimately to make me stronger. When the time is right, the situation will resolve one way or another.

Exercise

Stop reading and grab a pen. I want you to write down every negative thing in your life that you believe is there because someone else put it there. Then next to each bullet point I want you to come up with a new and positive spin that gives you 100% responsibility for the event. Now wait, let me be clear. There is a huge difference between blame and responsibility. I am not asking you to take the blame for the day you got mugged in broad daylight or the night your car got stolen. Fault and blame are pointless actions of the ego, blaming the mugger for attacking you doesn't undo the act of violence that occurred.

What I want you to do here is accept the situation as being a part of your life. You may not have chosen to have it happen, but for whatever reason it did. It's a part of you, and that means you are the only person who can heal it within yourself. Make peace with it and try to give yourself a point of view that does precisely zero finger pointing and has a high expectation that a positive outcome will result.

These exercises are very easily skipped and forgotten about, but please try to do them because they make a huge difference to the speed at which you can bring positive change into your life.

Chapter Three – I Want You, But I Don't Need You

"Through our eyes, the universe is perceiving itself. Through our ears, the universe is listening to its harmonies. We are the witnesses through which the universe becomes conscious of its glory, of its magnificence." - Alan W. Watts

It is common for people to get confused between what they want and what they need. It might sound like a subtle difference, but the outcomes you generate can be worlds apart. If you 'need' something then you are automatically coming at it from a position of weakness. For example, I 'need' oxygen to survive, if you take it away from me, it's a pretty big deal. It is fair to say that if I can't get ahold of a fairly constant supply of oxygen, it is going to put a fairly major crimp in my day. If somebody who can't swim falls into a lake, you see this neediness demonstrated with a reaction of panic to the situation.

However, I do not respond so dramatically to the knowledge that I do not have the speedboat that I 'want.' Not having a speedboat will not kill me and my life is not negatively affected by its absence in a dramatic or meaningful way, unless I believe I 'need' a speedboat to be happy.

'Need' is the cause of many failures, stress, and discontentment. People so often get attached to the illusion that happiness is a destination. They believe that if they would only get a better job, a better house, a faster car, and sexier partner, then suddenly life would be better somehow. Sadly, this is virtually never true. If you ask most people how much of an increase in salary they would need to be truly happy, the average response is to state that double the current amount would be fair and reasonable. However, as sure as night follows day; if you grant this wish and revisit the same person a few years later, they will still be unhappy, and likely still citing the amount of money they are paid as a reason. Happiness comes from within, and nothing external (including the numbers on your pay slip) can ultimately deliver the state you desire. Of course being happy and rich is a lot more exciting perhaps than being happy and poor, but we must get rid of the notion that it is the wealth that creates the desired state.

You see, the numbers that we state as being the catalyst for our happiness are entirely subjective and transient. If a guy who earns $30,000 a year believes that $60,000 would be the amount needed to be secure, and at the same time a guy at $50,000 believes that $100,000 is the magic number to deliver happiness, then which one of them is correct? Bearing in mind that both will more than likely return to dissatisfaction eventually.

The easiest way to witness the weakness of 'needing' is watching guys in a bar trying to pick up girls. You will notice that I frequently reference dating and attraction when I make my analogies, and it is because this environment best demonstrates men and women selling their heart out. I don't care how cold-hearted a guy is, landing a date with a stunningly beautiful woman is better than any sales bonus he will ever get. And it is because of this that most guys who dare to ask a woman for a date, start from a position of needing rather than wanting.

In any bar or club around the world, what is the single most commonly used line by guys hoping to pick up women? Yes, it is 'can I buy you a drink.' This is the default line for most guys attracted to a woman they do not know. It is a spectacularly weak approach and fails to achieve the desired result more than nine times out of ten. Have you ever wondered why, if this approach is so desperately poor and ineffective, that us guys continue to use it? The answer is in the 'needing,' or perhaps more specifically the desperation to avoid rejection. When a man sees a woman he likes, he opens himself up to being rejected—something us guys are particularly bad at dealing with.

Once you start worrying about being rejected, whether in a professional environment (such as making a sale) or personally approaching a man or woman you are attracted to, then you instantly place yourself lower on the totem pole of life than the other person. By offering to buy the lady a drink, he is stating that he does not believe what he has to offer as a male is enough to warrant her spending any time with him. Therefore, before they have even spoken he attempts to sweeten the deal for her by including a 'free drink.' If you are currently doing this yourself, stop it right now—it is insane!

Let me explain why this is so ridiculous. Imagine you are a car salesman, but you have so little faith in the automobiles you sell that as soon as a prospective buyer walks into your showroom, you run up to them and push a hundred bucks in their hand before begging them to take a look at the cars you have for sale. Do you think the prospect now believes that the cars here are amazing or do you agree they are more likely to be thinking 'boy these cars must be shit, I will pretend I am interested for a bit and then get out of here with my $100.'

About fifteen years ago, I interviewed for a job running a commercial radio station in Carlisle, England. Carlisle is a very small town in the middle of nowhere. It is close to the Scottish border, and the weather is terrible. While I am sure the people are lovely, I could not think of a single positive reason to justify moving my family several hundred miles to this part of the world. At the time I was only a deputy program director at another radio station in Preston. One day I was walking from my office to my car in the lot of the radio station when my cell phone rang with a number I did not recognize. I answered, and a woman introduced herself as the managing director of CFM, Carlisle. She said she had heard good things about me and would like to invite me to interview for their open program director vacancy. I was flattered, of course, and said I would travel up to meet her the following week.

I arrived at the radio station and was warmly greeted and given the tour of the studios before we sat down in the boardroom. It wasn't really like an interview at all, it was more like a chat with a friend. I answered honestly and casually, and even criticized various things I had heard the radio station doing. Not because I wanted to offend her or even because I was trying to impress her with my strength of character. I was telling her because I thought it was valuable feedback she could use, and I didn't particularly care if she agreed with me or not because I had already decided that Carlisle was not the place for my young family and me.

I left with mixed emotions, feeling like I had interviewed badly, very badly. I didn't want the job, but I felt like I had let myself down and left a bad impression with another leading professional in the UK media industry. However, later that night my cell rang again and the CFM Managing Director was jubilantly singing my praises and informing me how amazingly I had come across in the interview. She offered me the job then and there, detailed the generous bonus package and asked if I could start as soon as possible. She very disappointed when I said I would need to discuss the offer with my family, and that I would call her in the morning. I could tell she was crestfallen, but while I certainly did want to be a program director, I didn't need it so badly that I was prepared to move to the ass end of nowhere to get it.

The next morning, I called and informed her that I was flattered and appreciative, but would not be accepting the position. We ended the call politely, but without any of the previous day's pleasantries. From my point of view, that was the end of it, but CFM went on to make two further approaches with rapidly increasing salary and bonus packages. I was even accused of playing hard ball at the end. I wasn't; I just didn't need the job. Take food away from me, and we have a problem, take away my home and shelter, and I am going to struggle, but taking away a job in Carlisle has no real impact on my life.

Whether you are selling real estate, pitching for a promotion at work or asking a woman for a date, your attitude and mindset should always be, 'I want you, but I don't need you.' I'll wager that if you think back, you will be able to recall amazing things that happened to you when you weren't expecting them. Equally, you will have been in situations where you sold your heart out and got nowhere. When you are selling because you need just one more sale to hit your target, you are coming from a position of weakness, and your prospect can smell the fear on you like a cheap suit. When you approach a woman who you believe is out of your league, you better believe that she can see the fear in you before you say a single word. Your weakness is screaming out through your body language, the way you walk and the way you look at her.

Exercise

I want you to take a moment to review your goals in life. Ask yourself this. Are you chasing anything because you believe you need it to be happy, successful or to achieve some other label your ego is particularly attracted to? Do you want the Porsche because you think you need it to appear successful? Do you think you won't be happy at work until you get that promotion?

I want you to shift your thinking on these things. If you need something, then you probably are not going to get it anytime soon. Disconnect yourself from the outcome, and understand that you are perfect just as you are. Everything you need is already here—everything else is an accessory, and not getting it isn't going to kill you.

Chapter Four - Forgive Yourself First

"As I walked out the door toward the gate that would lead to my freedom, I knew if I didn't leave my bitterness and hatred behind, I'd still be in prison." - Nelson Mandela

It is almost a certainty that many years ago you buried some demons alive. The bad news is that these beasts don't die, they just change shape and eventually they invariably escape the grave. If you are holding onto any resentment, especially from your childhood, now is the time to let it go. Sometimes these issues are obvious, if you had an abusive childhood, then you probably have a very specific person in mind already. However, sometimes they are a little subtle, despite this, they are still capable of causing significant disruption to your inner state of peace. I am a good example of this latter situation.

Many years ago I recognized that I had two very profound issues. I had a very strong fear of rejection and also a fear of being constrained (not physically, but mentally restricted). It's always much easier to deal with a problem you know you have than to stumble around in the dark looking for the cause of your pain. However, what perplexed me with these specific problems was that I had no idea where they had come from. My childhood was as close to perfect as you could get. I was lucky enough to grow up with both sets of parents; I was loved and wanted for nothing. I simply couldn't understand why I was such a 'fuck up' in various areas of my life.

One day I was in a spiritual bookstore in New York, and I was talking to a woman who was also browsing the books on meditation. Her name was Anne, and she had such a peaceful aura about her. We ended up talking for about an hour, just standing there in this little store. We started to get into quite a deep territory as we talked about our lives, and I told her of this long-standing conundrum of mine.

She listened carefully and asked a few pertinent questions. Specifically, she wanted to know if my mother had been very strict or overbearing. I told her that was not the case at all, but that my dad used to infuriate me. He was a real no-nonsense sort of guy, and he always seemed to spoil my adventures by telling me the outcome before I had a chance to try them. I would get excited by a new project, sport or activity and he would spoil it by telling me that I would get bored with it within a week and it will all have been a waste of my time. The only thing I hated more than him doing that all the time, was the fact that he was virtually always correct.

When I turned thirteen, I couldn't take it anymore and I asked if my parents would pay for me to live at school. (My school had a small boarding contingency, as many students had parents who were serving in the armed forces.) I wanted to be around people my age and out from under the scrutiny of my father. I needed the freedom to make my mistakes and learn my own lessons. I told my parents what I wanted to do.

At this point in the story, Anne became very interested, "What did they say?" she inquired. When I told her they were fine about it and had stated that they would support whatever I wanted, Anne thought this was terrible.

"What? You mean they didn't even try to stop you?" she asked, with a very concerned expression. I told her again that they had not tried to stop me, and had just said I could do whatever I wanted.

Anne then explained that she felt this was surely the cause of my fear of rejection; that my parents didn't fight to keep me close. That it had been no hardship for them to be free of me at such a young age. I had never thought about it like that before, and I don't know if that is the only cause of my issue or not. However, since this revelation—and my acceptance of it—I have felt significantly more peaceful in almost every situation.

It doesn't matter whether you have huge hulking scars from immensely painful events, or just a collection of minor scrapes and dings, all must be forgiven before you can move on. This subject is worthy of a whole book by itself, and I can't do it justice in one chapter. However, I encourage you to address, this challenge as soon as possible.

Here are several things you can do that may help:

1. One of the most effective ways to address buried feelings about events and people from your past is a technique called Timeline Therapy. This is a talking therapy where you mentally revisit past traumatic events under the guidance of a trained counselor. Rather than experience all of the painful emotions again first hand, you are encouraged to view the event as a third person,

watching the situation unfold as though you are floating above it. This way you can detach yourself from the all-encompassing feelings you experienced at the time and try to see what was motivating the other person to treat you in such a way. It is good to remember that very few people are inherently evil, most negative behavior comes from fear in the other person. Bullies, for example, are the not super strong, tough individuals they appear to be, but are the opposite! Bullies are deeply afraid of something unspoken, and use violence and intimidation as a coping mechanism to try and suppress their distress.

2. Timeline Therapy would be my preference, but there is no doubt that any good, trained councilor will be able to help you release resentment and find peace with the traumatic events of your past through one of a several very effective methods. Perhaps you already know what your major fears and phobias are, and if so, you have already taken the first step towards a solution. So why not decide right now that you are going to take action and deal with this once and for all. Unless of course, your major demon is procrastination, then you'll probably just do it tomorrow, right?

3. Perhaps the easiest and most cost-effective solution can be found in the online member area of my VIP Club. Once you get started, you will get access to my Demon Slayer Hypnosis downloads. You will find a complete range of subliminal reprogramming tracks designed to deal with everything, including, fear of rejection, body confidence, and social anxiety issues.

Chapter Five - The Illusion of Permanency

Have you ever wondered how these hugely successful Hollywood stars—who appear to have everything in life that anyone could want—end up committing suicide? Despite their outward appearance, these people believe they are trapped in a situation that cannot ever get better, and their misery appears to be permanent.

Permanency does not exist in any form in our world. Everything living, everything nature placed here and everything we build will eventually crumble and fall. Nothing is saved; death and destruction are like the outward breath of God. He breathes in, and life is created, trees grown and buildings emerge. He breathes out, and people die, trees burn to the ground and buildings collapse.

Saddam Hussein spent a lifetime building as many statues in his image as possible, he commissioned hundreds of portraits to be painted and even officially named Iraq's main airport Saddam Hussein International Airport. He did all of this in a vain attempt to live on after his death, but he failed. Virtually all of the statues were pulled down and the airport renamed.

If you are pinning your happiness and success in life on achieving permanency in some way, then you are destined to fail. In your final days as you lay on your deathbed considering your vast property portfolio and the millions of dollars in the bank, most would happily trade it all for just one more week of life.

More subtly than that, we all also display our attachment to the idea of permanency when we give ourselves labels. Do you not think at some point when Adolf Hitler was growing up his mother sat him on her knee and told him he was such a good little boy. Was she wrong, or was right but perhaps only at that moment?

All too often we take these labels and decide that they are a permanent description of who we are.

- I am a good person (how do you know you always will be?)
- I am a fast sprinter (will that always be the case?)
- I have high standards, and will never stay in a hotel with less than a 5-star rating (Never?)

When I coach people one on one, they normally approach me with a label that they have decided is permanent. They come up to me and say, 'I am a terrible public speaker, I always make a fool of myself' or 'I have the worst bad luck, nothing ever goes right for me.'

If you believe there is anything about your life on this earth that is permanent, then I want you to spend some time thinking about how that could be true in a world where it is impossible. I apply this just as much to the 'good stuff' as the things we call 'bad.' I would call myself a 'good parent,' I love my children deeply and without question. However, I am willing to admit that at times I have made mistakes, given bad advice, shouted when I should have hugged and generally been a 'bad' parent. Especially during the challenging teenage years when my kids were striving to break free and be individuals. So which am I? 'A bad parent' or 'a good parent?' In reality, no label serves any useful purpose beyond the moment it is expressed.

Good times will end, and life will blindside you with events that spoil the fun. During periods of dark times, the storm will come to an end, and bright sunshine will once again fill your life. This is the ebb and flow of the universe— God will breathe in, and God will breathe out.

Chapter Six - Fear, Your New BFF

Fear keeps us focused on the past or worried about the future. If we can acknowledge our fear, we can realize that right now we are okay. Right now, today, we are still alive, and our bodies are working marvelously. Our eyes can still see the beautiful sky. Our ears can still hear the voices of our loved ones.
—Thich Nhat Hanh

That beautiful woman we talked about back in chapter four walks into a bar full of guys. Each man notices her, admires her and imagines himself with her. The married men allow a little sigh to escape their lips, and a few even curse the missed opportunity. But what of the single guys, surely here is a perfect chance to at least talk to a stunningly attractive woman. A small but perfectly formed window of opportunity to find out if her personality lives up to her beauty. In 99.9% of occasions, that woman will come and go without a single interaction—dozens of single guys deliberately opt out of the possibility of being her man on a daily basis… but why?

The answer is fear, while their heart says 'speak to her,' their head (meaning their ego) says:

- She is too hot for me.
- She probably has a boyfriend.
- She looks busy; I would be annoying her.
- I bet she gets hit on all the time and is sick of it.
- She will laugh in my face

The excuses and reasons are endless, and all of them are baseless, or if you prefer, false evidence appearing real… or fear. None of those excuses are a valid reason not to speak to this amazing girl. They are all just pieces of graffiti that are sprayed on the walls of your comfort zone. As we approach the edge of the zone, we notice that there are lots of brightly colored and aggressive looking warning signs. They scream that there is danger and risk beyond this point, and for your safety you should go no further!

Let's break down a couple of those excuses a little further:

She is too hot for me. Says who? Attraction is not a choice, we can't consciously make a decision to be attracted to someone or not— it just happens, or it doesn't. I have been in relationships with women who have been up to 15 years younger than me, but this does not mean all younger women are attracted to me. I wish, but sadly, this is not the case. Attraction is not a choice, I have been rejected more times than I can remember, but I don't take this personally, and I am certainly not offended by it. Failure is never in the rejection, but rather in the decision to take no action at all.

I have met truly awe-inspiring men and women over the years who describe themselves as, 'not that attractive.' Sometimes, I just want to grab them by their shirt collars and shake them until they see what I see. Only last month in London, I was coaching a financial executive who looked after billions of pounds worth of stock options on a daily basis. He is a partner in his firm, and quite quickly I gathered that he is a total genius at what he does. As we sat in a coffee shop off Knightsbridge, he relived the story of how he made his way from a council estate in Glasgow to a penthouse apartment in London worth over five million pounds. I was blown away by this guy and his story. As he came to the end of the tale, he looked me straight in the eye and said in his no-nonsense Scottish accent, 'shame I am such an ugly bastard right?' then laughed.

This brilliant guy considered himself to be unattractive and had spent most of the past decade either single or in a bad quality relationships that didn't serve him. In reality, he is an extremely intelligent, witty, charming and sophisticated man who has moved mountains to create pure success and abundance. I told him that there are millions of women on this planet who would think all their Christmases had come at once if they found a guy like him.

We are each our own worst critics, yet most of us ask ourselves important questions. Am I attractive? Am I a good person? What do I deserve in life? We should not be surprised when our answers to ourselves sound similar to those provided by the grumpy old men from the Muppets!

She probably has a boyfriend: Yes, this is a possibility, but are you saying that married people and those in long-term relationships no longer enjoy feeling attractive to other people?

I don't know about you, but I have found that it is often the married and long-term relationship gang who get the least compliments in life. If I see someone I find attractive; I always make a point of going out of my way to tell them so. Quite often, they will be shocked and blurt out, 'Oh, I'm married, sorry.' I will just say, 'I know,' then smile and walk away. My intention was not to do anything other than making their day just a little brighter.

If you are not speaking to people you are attracted to because you are afraid you will get rejected because they are in a relationship, then you have this whole thing the wrong away around. You are not supposed to be pushing through your comfort zone to get something—such as a phone number, a date or even sex—but rather to give something. You have the power to make everyone you meet—regardless of gender—feel amazing, unique and special. To not use this wonderful power is a crime, and everyone concerned is robbed of joy undelivered.

Occasionally, people are so used to living in a loveless world that they refuse to accept this gift from you. It happened to me even yesterday, I was in the bank, and one of the most stylish women I have ever seen in my life walked in. She must have spent over four hours getting ready that day—she looked amazing. As is my custom, I walked over to her and said, 'Excuse me, I just wanted to let you know that you look amazing.' I smiled and expected something resembling a smile in return—I didn't get it. She curled up her lip, looked me straight in the eye, glaring, and said, 'Go away.'

There was no point in taking offense because I didn't have enough data to understand why she reacted like that. Perhaps she was just dumped by her boyfriend, maybe she lost her job that morning, or maybe she was just in one hell of a bad mood and everyone was getting a snarly response that day. Who knows? But what I do know is that the problem does not belong to me, unless I choose to make it so by being offended or taking her reaction personally.

Yes, it is true that if you always obey the warning signs nailed to the outer walls of your comfort zone, you will be protected from awkward situations like the one I just described. But you will also never experience the flip side of that scenario. I have amazing friends all over the world because I make strangers feel great on purpose. I consider the world to be my playground; I believe I can travel alone anywhere on the planet and leave having had a fabulous time with a whole new group of friends.

I want this to be a tool you can use to release you from the life-limiting and defeating loops created by fear. When we use the word fear, we normally apply it to situations where we wrongly or rightly predict that we are at risk of harm. For example, standing on the edge of a tall building generates a sensation of fear and anxiety, so we become acutely aware of what could happen if we act up in those situations. We can be afraid before a job interview because we have become attached to a particular outcome and don't want to experience rejection followed by the loss of that outcome. Remember, however, that fear usually isn't this obvious or dramatic, but it can still be a hugely limiting factor in our lives.

When people go on a diet, they start out with good intentions and a desperate desire to improve the way they look and feel. An honorable pursuit, but why do nearly 95% of them end up not only putting back on all the weight they lost in the first place, plus an additional few pounds for good measure? The answer is fear. At the start of the diet, the pain of looking in the mirror or not being able to squeeze into their favorite jeans anymore creates low-level fear. What if I just keep getting bigger? What if I have nothing to wear to the party? What if they start calling me names at school? So, we launch the diet motivated to move our chubby body away from the fear. Then we lose a bit of weight, and the original fear subsides, but it is often replaced by a new concern. You see, we enjoy our tasty treats and take-out in front of a good movie. Suddenly, we feel like we are depriving ourselves of some of the fun bits of life we've enjoyed. We fear that if we carry on being strict with ourselves, we are going to be short-changed by life and have less fun. Thus begins the yo-yo diet routine that dominates the life of so many good people.

I am writing this section of the book in the business class cabin of a British Airways flight from London Heathrow to Austin, Texas and even here fear is present. I am not talking about worrying about the plane crashing or running into some scary turbulence. I have been on board for just two hours, and so far I have been offered free alcohol at least half a dozen times. I can't drink alcohol because it has a nasty habit of trying to kill me. If you have read my book Alcohol Lied to Me, you will know that I had a near two decade-long battle with booze and I became a teetotaler about six or seven years ago. I don't have to struggle to stay away from drinking, no part of me wants to go back to where I was, but there is an element of fear at the back of my head every time the flight attendant comes down the aisle with the trolley. I turn down a very expensive French Bordeaux and instead ask for a cheap glass of water. The northerner in me feels like I am getting ripped off—I feel like I am getting a much poorer value for my money than the guy next to me who has knocked back $100 worth of wine and brandy so far. I am 99% certain that I won't buckle in the name of value, but I am acutely aware and afraid of that 1% still lingering in the back of my mind.

Fear is present on a daily basis and in a myriad of ways. We are taught to be careful, to listen to fear and respond accordingly, and the vast majority of society obeys this unwritten law. The result is a safer, more boring and less fulfilling life. This is the world of the Average Joe and the Average Jane—safe and steady, but beige. What I am encouraging you to do is respond to fear in a highly counter-intuitive way. Instead of seeing fear as a warning, I want you to see it as an opportunity light blinking on the dashboard of your life. Essentially, if you are afraid of it, then you must do it!

I can't begin to tell you how many people I meet who are full of regret, and it is virtually never about the things they have done in their life. Much more common are regrets about the things they didn't do. The last time I saw my aunty Angela, she had a coffee with my parents at their home in Darlington. I joined them all for a short while, and as I sat down, Angela was expressing her regret that she had never learned to drive. She had started to learn but got too afraid to ever put in for the test, and it just became one of those things we label shoulda, woulda, coulda. Two years previously, Angela had sadly been diagnosed with C.U.P. cancer (cancer of unknown primary origin). She was still her old lively self, but her prognosis was not great, all treatment had ultimately failed. The doctors estimated she had between six and nine months to live. Angela decided that before it became impossible, she was going to take and pass her driving test.

She never got the chance, as she died three weeks later. The moment she died, passing or failing that driving test became irrelevant; as did all the fear about taking the test in the first place. There are dozens of things that you want but don't have because fear is preventing you from going after them. One day in the future all that fear will be rendered pointless by the same event that Angela went through, the event that no one has ever managed to avoid. What I am saying is that your ego is trying to protect you from harm by encouraging you to avoid risk by using fear as a virtual 2x4 to hit you over the head with.

Your body is like an apartment shared between two tenants. The ego and the soul, or if you prefer, the conscious mind and the unconscious mind. These are the tenants of your body. The soul is eternal and divine, it is essentially a fragment of God and it knows this for certain. It is also acutely aware that the apartment it is renting is temporary, and when the lease ends it will just move to a new place and start over. However, the ego knows that when the lease ends that's the end of the story, its game over. This creates a sensation of blind panic for the ego, which just flat refuses to accept the situation. It kicks and screams trying to prove that it can prevent the lease from ending. Hey perhaps if you fill the apartment with more and more stuff, and then never leave so they can't come in and dump your possessions, then perhaps the lease will continue evermore, right? The ego is so terrified of the end; it has been rendered insane by the constant thought of it.

Out of this insanity, we get all the self-limiting beliefs that hold us back.

- Save for a rainy day.
- What can go wrong, will go wrong.
- She's too hot for you; she will reject you.
- You are not ready for your driving test.
- You are not good enough for that promotion at work.

The ego uses the past as a reverse projector in an attempt to control the uncontrollable. Fear is liberally applied to all areas of your life with the hope that it will keep you safe, albeit completely unfulfilled. You are alive but miserable, that's good enough. The ego doesn't particularly care how happy you are; its primary focus is trying in vain to avoid the inevitable final act, at whatever cost.

What I am about to ask you to do is acknowledge that one of your tenants is insane, and while you can't evict, you can decide to stop listening to his/her insane ramblings. From this point on, fear should be seen as the screams in the night of your troublesome tenant. All the predictions of doom, gloom, terror, and trauma are nothing more than a desperate illusion.

Start living in the knowledge that the only moment that exists is this one, right here and right now. The past and the future do not exist and they never will—this is it, and this is all there will ever be.

There is a percentage chance that this nineteen-year-old Boeing 777-200 aircraft will crash before I reach Austin, Texas—so should I just stop writing now just in case? No, of course not, because right here at this moment I am alive, and as long as that situation continues I have a message to deliver.

Exercise:

I want you to stop reading at this point and take a little life inventory. Grab a pen and paper and write down everything you can think of that you have ever wanted to achieve but have been prevented from doing so by fear. Perhaps you have always wanted to skydive, but can't quite bring yourself to sign up for a jump. Maybe there is a senior position opening at work, and you have told yourself that you are not quite ready and might try again in a few years. Perhaps you have been head over heals in love with Nicola in reception for years and never done anything about it?

On a blank piece of paper draw four columns, in the first column write your goal, in the second write down how fear is preventing you from achieving this goal, in the third column write down what will happen if you continue to let fear dominate this area of your life. In the final column, I want you to imagine how you would feel if you ignored the 'Danger, Do Not Pass' signs hanging on the wall of your comfort zone and charged on through regardless.

One of the most positive motivational speakers that America ever produced was Zig Ziglar. He would describe the start of his day in such a beautiful way. He used to say, 'Every morning at 6 am my opportunity clock would go off and wake me up. I don't call it an alarm clock because that's negative. That bell signals the start of a whole new day full of fantastic opportunities.'

Chapter Seven – Outcomes & Labels

"By taking the time to stop and appreciate who you are and what you've achieved—and perhaps learned through a few mistakes, stumbles and losses—you actually can enhance everything about you. Self-acknowledgment and appreciation are what give you the insights and awareness to move forward toward higher goals and accomplishments", - Jack Canfield

This book is designed to profoundly change your life, in just the same way the knowledge I share in it changed mine. It took me thirty years of struggling to swim upstream in life before I discovered the secrets in these books. I was an overweight, alcohol addicted and angry man who never quite lived up to his potential. I suffered depression, anxiety, and low self-esteem for many, many years. No matter how much money I earned, no matter how much I drank, no matter how many things I bought, the vacuum inside me just kept growing bigger and bigger.

Since I discovered the material you are about to read, I have lost over sixty pounds, quit drinking, given up my boring office job (to follow my dream of being a full-time author), and moved to a beautiful island in the Mediterranean that boasts three hundred days of sunshine a year. I am forty-one years old, and these days I step out of my villa pick up my surfboard and spend my days on the beach with the girl of my dreams. Yes, I am insufferably annoying to be friends with on Facebook… and you will be too!

Forget all that 'positive thinking' nonsense, and the 'get rich quick' notions of the 'law of attraction' and other such new age bandwagon chasers. Yes, you can have everything in life you want, but I will warn you here and now! The chances are high, better than good at least, that what you are here to do, what that vacuum inside you needs to be filled with, is a million miles away from what you currently think you need.

Just as a building without a foundation will not be habitable, you cannot turn your world around and start living an exceptional life with just the click of your fingers. Books and gurus are claiming that things like the 'law of attraction' and 'reality creation' are easy, simply aren't telling the truth. Sure, on paper it may appear to be easy, but the same is true when I watch my mother bake and decorate a beautiful wedding cake. As I watch the icing and decorative piping almost jump right onto the cake, it seems like the easiest thing in the world.

However, I know that the flow, expertise, and precision of my mother's hands are all the direct result of decades of experience, doing this intricate artwork over and over again. I don't need to attempt to replicate her work to know that it would be an abomination in my hands. Yes, in theory, getting the exceptional life you dream about is easy, but only if you have changed your whole mindset and approach to life first—and this part is not easy.

'Thoughts become things' is an often-quoted saying, and is a cornerstone of books such as The Secret. The principle is simple; you get what you think about the most. So, if you think like a wealthy person, you will become rich, think like an ex-drinker and you will stop drinking, and so on. There is a slight problem with this theory—it is completely wrong and doesn't work! Let me tell you why; thoughts are predominately generated by your ego (the insane part of your mind), but the ego doesn't have the power to manifest (or attract, if you prefer). A single thought in and of itself is powerless unless it becomes a belief.

Essentially, thoughts are conscious (weak), and beliefs are subconscious (powerful).

For example, you don't have to constantly remind yourself not to jump off tall buildings—you have a deeply embedded belief that this would be dangerous and most likely fatal behavior. Your subconscious protects you from the wild rambling desires of your ego by ignoring virtually everything it says. This is a very good thing—how many times have you caught yourself wishing harm to someone who has hurt you in some way (a cheating ex or a pressuring boss) only to calm down and realize violence wouldn't have helped. If your subconscious listened to every command of your ego, chances are you would be reading this from inside a prison cell, perhaps with me as your cellmate.

Exercise

I would like you to spend one week doing something significant. I want you to become aware of your ego. It's imperative that you recognize where your desires and motivations are coming from. The reason we do this is to reduce the power of this part of you, to make space for you to hear the silence of your subconscious. In that silence is the answer to all of your most key questions, we just never stop to listen to what is waiting to be said. In fact, most people go their entire lifetime without ever hearing the message that could have changed their life. The voice of the ego is so constant that we come to believe that this is who we are. But this voice in our head passing judgment and making demands is NOT who we are, it is merely an illusion.

But how do I know when my ego is speaking?

This is simple—any thought or statement that begins with 'I' is the voice of your ego!

- I drive a Mercedes.
- I only stay in 5-star hotels.
- I need a drink in the evening to help me relax.
- I won't accept people disrespecting me.
- I don't think she is good enough for him.
- I expect good service when I dine out.
- I deserve the promotion more than him.

We all think we know who we are, but really, most of the things that we decide to label ourselves with are purely statements of the ego. Even positive labels—'I am a great parent,' 'I am a dedicated employee,' or 'I am a loyal and reliable friend,'—all these pronouncements come from a part of our mind that is unstable. The ego lives only in the conscious mind, and every time you make a statement that begins with the word 'I,' you can be sure it was created by some false belief in this part of your physical being.

All statements of 'I' are subjective, and as such is pointless. Our body and mind are not who we are; they are just things we own for a short while. When people ask me what I do for a living, I answer by saying, 'I am an author.' But is that really who I am? I think not. The ego cannot cope with having questions left unanswered, so we are forced to find comfort in applying a label to describe our reason to be…the point of our existence. Then we become attached to this security blanket and set about embedding it deeper into our identification with life. Photographers get up each morning and take photographs—because that's what the label dictates. This is how we can spend an entire lifetime avoiding the point of life. Eventually, we become so attached to the name that our ego tries to own it. We start to compete with other people who have selected the same direction. We need proof that we are the best, first, quickest or any other illusionary piece of evidence that suggests we have achieved permanency in our label.

A person might proudly declare, 'I give generously to charity, I am a good person.' We know this pronouncement is the pointless bleating of the ego. Money is relative if a billionaire makes a million dollar donation, and at the same time a homeless man gives ten bucks, all the money he has—who is the more generous. The correct answer is neither, because any judgment on that is still just an assessment of the ego, which, as we have already established, is insane!

All pain and suffering are created directly by this part of us and by our insistence on laying claim to labels. On a personal level, it can be felt in the sensation of jealously we experience when our neighbor pulls into his driveway with a brand new sports car. On a global level, it has been demonstrated countless times when nations declare war on each other. Mostly, these acts of violence erupt when one country attempts to take something that another country has declared as its own.

The ego is tiny and yet believes itself to be big and powerful. The subconscious is infinite but believes nothing at all. It feels no need to question or judge, it simply does.

We are prevented from consciously accessing the limitless and divine power of our subconscious because we can't be trusted not to act like power crazy, narcissistic idiots. Apart from that, we would most likely kill ourselves in seconds, as the ego assures us that it knows what it is doing as it lifts the hood on the engine that beats our heart and fills our lungs with air. This is the same voice that assures us that we don't need to read the instruction manual when we buy a new piece of electronic equipment or flat pack furniture. I don't trust this voice any more than I trusted my friend at school who insisted that washing powder has the same effect as cocaine. He spent the afternoon in the hospital foaming from the nose.

We can only access the power of the subconscious by two very different methods. Firstly, it can be achieved through a lifetime of deep meditation and constant cleaning of the mind. Most people don't have the patience or dedication to take this route. However, the second course is practiced by all of us, and we do it every day. Repetition is how we fool the gatekeeper of the subconscious into allowing us access to this amazing super computer. The conscious mind is so limited that it can only complete one task at a time, and so when we do something often enough, the mind creates a physical pathway to complete this function automatically, thus freeing up processing power for other tasks. This would be a fantastic benefit of the human mind if we only did things that were founded in love and respect for ourselves and others. For example, what if you started a routine of ringing your mother at 9 am each morning and telling her that you love her. After a while, you would not even have to think about it, at 9 am you would gravitate to the phone and start dialing, even if you were thinking about doing something completely different.

Sadly, we don't always tend to use this power for good. We prefer to repeatedly stick cigarettes in our mouths, eat junk food and drink alcohol until we are sick. These are the programs that we allow to inadvertently bleed though into our subconscious. Once past the gatekeeper and inside, there are no further filters to protect us, as this part of the mind does not judge or question, it only completes.

The ego loves something else apart from these labels… outcomes! When we get attached to a specific outcome, we create the possibility of failure. It is not possible to fail at anything until we decide, subjectively, what failure looks like. Sometimes even when we get the outcome that we have pre-decided will indicate that we were successful, we still end up miserable. For example, about a decade ago I successfully interviewed for a director level position running a large regional radio station in the North East of England. In my head, landing this job was a success and failing to get the position was a terrible thing. I got the outcome I had pre-decided as being 'good' and went on to have eighteen months of the most miserable time in my life working for this radio station. For six months of that time, I was under the care of a doctor suffering from severe anxiety and stress. Ridiculously, if I had 'failed' to land this job, I would have beaten myself up and felt miserable. I would have been blissfully unaware how much pain and misery my 'failure' had saved me.

The ego thinks it is an expert at predicting the future, but in reality, the ego is as adept at fortune telling as I am at ballet dancing, and yet we still listen to it. Again, I remind you of what we talked about in chapter four, it is fine to want something, but as soon as you get attached to a specific outcome and then need that to happen, you are in dangerous territory. For example, if you get the opportunity to pitch a sale to a huge client, and you find yourself daydreaming about what you are going to do with the massive bonus check that will surely follow. You can probably see how easily the more you think about this, the more you get attached to the outcome. Eventually, you turn a beautiful opportunity in your life into a trap door. Your attachment to the outcome and your need to make the sale become a potential source of pain and misery in your life.

Instead, try to be open to wherever the universe wants to take you on this journey. It may be that failing to make the sale on this pitch will be the making of your career. It could be that if you made this sale, it would lead to you neglecting your other clients and eventually losing your job, or you could be right and it could just be a big pay day for you and your family. The point is, you don't know and so unless you want to keep on creating trap doors for yourself, accept that the universe has a plan for you and that beautiful things are coming whether you like it or not.

Thank you for reading Zero Limits with me, if you have enjoyed this book, please do take a few minutes to go back to the online store you bought it from and leave a rating and review.

If you are ready to invest in your personal and professional success, don't forget to check out my VIP coaching program at www.CraigBeck.com

Good Luck & Best Wishes

Craig Beck

Recommended links
- http://www.CraigBeck.com
- http://www.SubAttraction.com
- http://www.PowerfullyConfident.com

LAW OF ATTRACTION
UNIVERSITY

Are You Serious About This?

Do you want to be the next person to start living the life of their dreams?

www.craigbeck.com

Life is harsh right? But if you work long and hard you can ease the struggle... no pain, no gain!

Wrong, wrong, wrong! Virtually everything you have been told about how to have a happy, successful life is wrong. Not just a little bit wrong, but the exact polar opposite of the truth!

So many people spend an entire lifetime not quite having enough... they get stuck in a job they don't like, in a relationship that isn't healthy and struggle along, always with not quite enough money.

Life is not meant to be a struggle, and money is not supposed to be scarce. You are not here to spend half your precious time on this planet working in a job that doesn't fulfill you, and worse, leaves you wondering just what the point of it all is!

• Yes, I know you read 'The Secret' and it didn't work the way you hoped.
• Yes, I know you tried positive thinking and found it impossible to maintain.
• Yes, I know you have read self-help books and a hundred other things.

Why didn't any of that work and why don't you have the life you dream of?

The truth has been sanitized to appeal to a mass market—remember, what I am about to show you flies in the face of what virtually everyone currently believes. Only a select will be open minded enough to be able to process this knowledge.

I do not advertise this website. Most people never find this coaching program. There is a reason you are here. You should trust me on this because a uniquely magical experience is just a mouse click away. Why not decide now and join my Manifesting Magic Coaching Program today?

I want you to be the next person whose life completely changes… beyond their wildest dreams.

www.CraigBeck.com

www.ingramcontent.com/pod-product-compliance
Lightning Source LLC
Chambersburg PA
CBHW021548200526
45163CB00016B/3023